® Landoll, Inc.
Ashland, Ohio 44805
LOONEY TUNES, characters, names, and all related
indicia are trademarks of Warner Bros., Inc. © 1997.
No part of this book may be reproduced or copied.
All Rights Reserved. Made in the U.S.A. LAN229

STORYBOOK
Full Moon Feline

by Charles Carney

Illustrated by Sol Studios, Argentina and Landoll, Inc.

In the space station on the moon, lunar pioneers had all the comforts of home: books, television, a laser disc player, a popcorn popper, easy chairs, electronic games, a cat, and a canary.

But the experiment was complete, and the pioneers were called back to Earth. As the last shuttle blasted off from the shadowy face of the moon, one astronaut said to his partner. "Have you seen that crazy cat?"

Sylvester, who was sleeping on top of the warm power generator, peeked over the edge of the space station window. He blinked away the sleep and watched . . .

. . . as the spaceship took off from the moon and grew smaller, and smaller. He stared at the harsh gray lunar landscape. *Uh-oh*, he thought. This could be a real problem.

Then, from somewhere deep inside the space station, he heard singing, and his heart soared. *Sufferin' succotash!* he thought. *They forgot the bird, too!*

Sylvester crept s-l-o-w-l-y on his belly into the aviary. *Jeepers*, Sylvester said to himself. They had to teach him to sing *opera*? High above the floor, Tweety sang happily in his little cage.

WHOOSH! A black and white blur swung by on a vine and reached for Tweety. "I tawt I taw a puddy tat!" he said. Then it went by in the opposite direction. "I *did* taw a puddy tat—who want to pway with me!"

As the cat grabbed for him, Tweety reached out and cut the vine. CRAAASH! BOOM! CLATTER! "Awww—the poor puddy tat faw down, go BOOOM!" Tweety said sweetly.

Sylvester drummed his fingers on the floor and his stomach began to growl like an engine without any oil. He heard Tweety singing in the kitchen and chuckled. He had a plan.

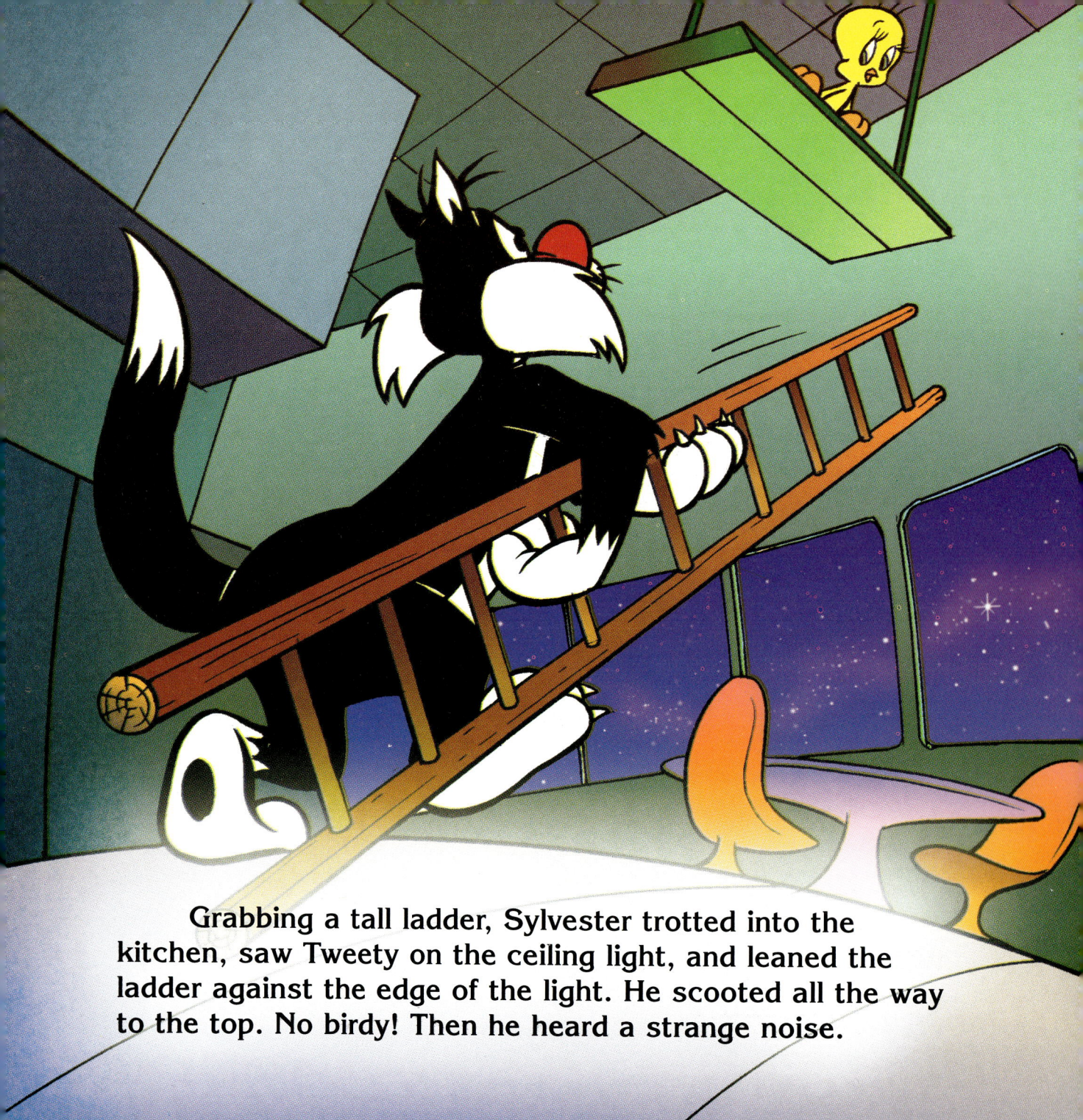

Grabbing a tall ladder, Sylvester trotted into the kitchen, saw Tweety on the ceiling light, and leaned the ladder against the edge of the light. He scooted all the way to the top. No birdy! Then he heard a strange noise.

Tweety pushed a tub of water next to the ladder, then took a saw to the ladder's bottom rung. Sylvester ran up the ladder. One by one the rungs of the ladder went CRACK! and SNAP! till he was standing on just two very long pieces of wood. Luckily, cats have excellent balance.

Sometimes.

And they hate water. Almost as much as they hate smart little birdies. But Sylvester had more than one lunch plan.

He put on a bird suit. "Here, birdy-birdy. The babysitter's here, come to play a game with the little squab (and the loser gets eaten)!"

"Let's pway ball, puddybirdy!" said Tweety, flying out of the space station's HONEY PRODUCTION CHAMBER with a huge beehive. Tweety bounced the hive, making the bees inside very angry. Then he dropped it into Sylvester's birdy suit pants.

"Yeeeooowww!" Sylvester screamed as the angry bees swarmed around the inside of his bird pants. Up and down! Left and right he hopped! "Hi-ho puddybirdy!" Tweety called out.

    Hiding in the garden, Sylvester had another idea. He grabbed the birdbath basin, leaned back, and stuck it into his mouth, then Tweety stepped in for a bath. "Aah! A bubble bath!" the little canary said, making soap bar suds. Sylvester sputtered and gurgled bubbles, but he stayed still. He would eat this troublemaker yet.

"And this water is too cold," Tweety said, pulling out a big, whistling teapot and dumping the boiling water into the birdbath. "That's better!"

"Aaaaaagh!" screamed Sylvester, shoving a fire hose into his mouth and turning on the water.

"Fire in the puddy tat! Fire in the puddy tat!" Tweety yelled. He put on a fireman's hat and turned on the hose all the way. The water squirted poor Sylvester across the garden, out the door, and down a long hallway.

Sylvester crept up to the GRAVITY SIMULATOR on his tiptoes. Inside, hanging from the high ceiling, was a small cage for experiments, where Tweety sat singing. Sylvester couldn't stand opera.

He shut the door, turned the controls to ZERO GRAVITY, and floated like a balloon. Pulling out two pieces of bread, he ordered Tweety to get in. Tweety shook his head "no."

The cat pulled out a mallet. Tweety pulled out a remote control and pointed to the gravity switch below. Sylvester shook his head. "No!" Click!

Sylvester slammed to the floor. Click! He flew to the ceiling. Click! Floor! Click! Ceiling! Click! Floor!

Sylvester got out as he heard the roar of a space shuttle docking to the space station. "Rescued!" he squealed. "Somebody save me from that canary!" he screamed, running into a pet carrier cage and locking the door. "Whew!" Then he heard a throat clear.

Behind him stood two tough-looking bulldogs, one flipping a coin. "Lookin' for somethin', kitty boy?" one of the dogs said, nastily. Then there was a terrible scuffle.

Tweety watched from his new perch a few feet away. "I wose more puddy tat pwaymates that way!" he said.